HA-RIKUD

The Jewish Dance

HA-RIKUD

The Jewish Dance

edited by

FRED BERK

AMERICAN ZIONIST YOUTH FOUNDATION

UNION OF AMERICAN HEBREW CONGREGATIONS

Library of Congress Cataloging in Publication Data

Berk, Fred, 1911-   comp.
   Ha-Rikud.

   SUMMARY: The history of Jewish folk dance is accompanied by directions for
twenty-five Israeli folk dances and suggestions for starting a folk dance group.
   1. Dancing—Jews—Juvenile literature. 2. Folk dancing, Israeli—Juvenile literature. [1. Folk dancing, Israeli] I. Title. II. Title: Ha-Rikud: the Jewish Dance.
GV1703. P3B43   793.3'1   72-3572

Foreword

Manifold ethnic, religious, and cultural impressions upon the texture of Israeli life—woven out of the unique and sturdy warp of Jewish heritage and a richly blended weft of Jewish diversity—are strikingly manifest in the dances of the nation. In but one generation of statehood, Israel's dance forms have become a hallmark of her people and a part of the daily life of Jews worldwide.

Jewish youths especially have responded with deeper identity and Jewish consciousness to the full-range of Jewish experience expressed in Israeli folk dances. In the United States and Canada it is rare that informal get-togethers, formal conferences, holidays, and organized programs involving Jewish youth groups do not include the camaraderie, the chaverut of Hebrew songs and Israeli dances.

The American Zionist Youth Foundation welcomes the co-publication of an anthology of Jewish dance that traces the development of the folk dance in Israel and documents its special significance for the young in America and in Israel. The foundation provides to American Jewish youths consultation and program services that encourage the intensification of their Jewishness and their Zionist convictions. Fred Berk's unusual collection of dances, identifying the multiplicity of influences that created the Jewish dance in Israel, contributes to this purpose by enhancing knowledge and appreciation of Jewish history, Jewish mores, and the Jewish homeland. We commend him for the success of his endeavor.

Recognizing the expanding interest in folk dancing among young people in the United States and the role it plays for Jewish youth, AZYF has initiated dance projects, such as the Israel Summer Dance Institute and the Leadership Training Seminar, in addition to sponsorship of an annual New York City-wide Israel Folk Dance Festival that has led to the production of similar dance festivals in other American cities. Fred Berk, a gifted and dedicated artist, director of the Israel Folk Dance Institute under AZYF auspices, has inspired these dance programs. His manual will serve as another source of inspiration.

William Levine
Executive Director
American Zionist Youth Foundation

Introduction

Dancing has been called the "mother of the arts." And so it is if the discovery of ancient cave paintings in northern Spain tells us anything. These paintings, drawn about 50,000 years ago, depict people in dancing positions. Evidently the dance was of primary importance in the life of primitive peoples and ancient civilizations. It is the oldest of the arts and undoubtedly the most ancient form of religious expression. Before feelings and beliefs were articulated in words, the rhythm and movement of the body served the purpose of communicating and interpreting fears, joys, and beliefs.

Records of antiquity tell us that the dance was connected with every significant event in the life of an individual and a people. Dancing was a vital part of all rites de passage: birth, acceptance into a tribe, marriage, and death. In addition to the life cycle, the important occasions in the cycle of the years were marked by dancing. And the third form of dance was expressed in relation to important events in the life of the people such as military triumphs, even defeats.

The same kinds of dance expression are found in Jewish history. According to the Jewish Encyclopedia, "religious dance constituted the principal feature of every festival." (iv, 425) The Bible indicates many instances when dance was definitely a "principal feature." At the Red Sea, Miriam and her maidens danced in joy; the Israelites danced before the golden calf; the women danced when David returned from slaying Goliath; and David himself danced ecstatically before the Ark of the Covenant. Dancing was a feature of the temple services, and Koheleth reminds us that there is indeed, for most occasions that are deeply meaningful, a "time to dance."

So today there is a time to dance for the expression of our religious feelings and beliefs. Thus we are pleased to co-publish this manual of instruction on Jewish dancing by the master teacher, Fred Berk. We hope that by learning the various patterns and movements, our students will come to appreciate the dance as a beautiful and authentic form of religious expression for the home, the camp, the school, and the synagogue.

Jack D. Spiro, Director
Commission on Jewish Education
UAHC-CCAR

Contents

Illustrations follow page 31

PART I

History

1 The Beginning of Jewish Dancing

BENJAMIN ZEMACH

Benjamin Zemach, internationally known director and choreographer, is the brother of the famed Nahum Zemach, founder of the Habimah Theater.

He directed many plays and dance productions in New York, Canada, on the West Coast, and in Israel, staged ballets for the Hollywood Bowl, was dialogue and dance director for motion pictures at RKO and Universal Studios.

In 1955, he spent one year in Israel at the invitation of the Habimah to direct their drama workshop studio. Presently he is directing the drama-dance department at the University of Judaism in Los Angeles.

The language of dance is older than human language itself since body movement was used for communication before sound. When we study primitive peoples, we see that the dance was the first of all their methods of expression. The dance roused their spirits for battle against their enemies and was used to pray for rain to fructify their fields and increase their harvests. There were joyous dances used both to inspire hunters before their departure and to welcome them when they returned with their spoils. The love and marriage dances indicate that primitive peoples also expressed their more intimate feelings primarily through dancing. However, dance as a form of distraction did not exist. It was designed as part of the people's private and collective lives.

The Jews, too, had dances for all their different needs in biblical days. In the Bible and the Talmud there are many synonyms for dance: *machol, rikud, pazos, dalogi, ditza, kafotz, sachek, chagog.*

A wide field of Jewish dance activity stands before us if we succeed in clarifying the basic features of Jewish dance forms in biblical times. Many peoples, including Americans, seek for the essentials of modern dance primarily among primitive dance forms, and in order to make progress we must draw sustenance from the living well of the Jewish dance.

In biblical times, dance activity took place concurrently with important national events. Cymbals of various forms were popular in the time of Miriam, the prophetess, and King David. Jeremiah, speaking of the coming national revival of the Jewish people, said, "You will don cymbals and go forth in joyous dancing." We come across the cymbal in the time of Saul who was met by a group of prophets carrying flutes, cymbals, and string instruments.

It is known that ceremonial processions, such as those attendant on the sacrifices and the convocation of the people with trumpets, were accompanied by various dance movements. The temple had a company of approximately four thousand musicians, among them many different directors. At each ceremonial procession—removing the ashes, the sacrifice on Yom Kippur and on other holidays,[1] while kneeling—dance movements took place and, through these, people expressed their deepest spiritual feelings in prayers and homage to the Almighty.

In King David's time, the dance in front of the ark provided another example of processional dance to choral accompaniment. We assume that the dance began when the people were absolutely silent, in an awed trance, at which point the music would slowly begin to crescendo and turn into a joyous dance which evolved into jumping and, subsequently, into choral dancing.

Private and nature festivals exhibited the same development. The Bible tells of Samson's marriage which was celebrated for thirty days. There were psalms of praise while pressing the grapes and while harvesting the corn. All such nature festivals, with their accompanying dances, were an expression of love for the soil, an appreciation for a joyful and fertile life, a bubbling song of the harvest.

The Jewish concept of monotheism tended to mold diverse parts into one great unity. Jewish folk dance was also affected by this tendency and, although each dance had its own individual movements, Jewish dance has an overall architectural harmony and a unified form.

Primitive Jewish dance came as a natural expression of spiritual life. The ecstasy of the prophets and their enthusiastic body movements were not an ecstasy of weakness, of visionary illness, but rather an ecstasy of moral truth, of inner excitement, of clear vision. Prophetic ecstasy never extended to the masochistic rituals practiced by the surrounding heathen cults. They did not beat each other with sticks and other instruments in order to induce artificial excitement and create an abnormal state. It was forbidden to induce ecstasy through artificial means. It had come as a result of deep joy and personal need. The only thing permitted was musical instruments which were used to accompany dance movements.

In biblical times the religious nature festivals were very colorful. A good example is provided by the water festivals which were generally accompanied by torch dances. It is thought that the torch dances were introduced by the Romans when they invaded Palestine. The water parade was another genuine folk spectacle. It began with a procession from Mount Moriah to Lake Shileah. At its head marched the priest holding a golden pitcher with which he drew water to pour on the altar. On the return journey he stopped at the water gate where the people met him to the accompaniment of silver trumpets and the song: "And Ye Shall Draw Water with Joy from the Wells of Salvation."

Another group of priests went to Motza and brought back willow rods. The branches were placed on the altar and the priest sprinkled them with water from the golden pitcher, after which the procession carried the branches around the altar. The Levites used to sing "Hallel" and the people accompanied them and shook their palm branches to the rhythm of the music.

On that evening the men were admitted to one of the large halls in the temple normally reserved for women. The women were seated on the roof and in the galleries. The columns were decorated with golden candelabras fifteen yards high. Young priests stood on ladders near the candelabras and constantly added oil from large pitchers. The flames became increasingly brighter and the torch dance began. The most respected personalities of Jerusalem would dance with torches in their hands. They would bend their bodies in rhythm and throw their torches up and catch them before they hit the ground.

What do we know concerning Jewish dance in later eras?

We know that the ceremonial dances ceased with the cessation of other forms of public Jewish life. Ceremonial dances could no longer exist when Jewish life began to be suppressed among the peoples of the Diaspora. The expulsion of the Jews from their own soil marked the end of their nature festivals. Jewish life was restricted to home and synagogue. There remained only echoes, symbolizing the glorious past. Parts of the folk festivals were zealously observed by the Jewish people. It is sufficient to point to the *lulav* (palm branch) and *etrog* (citrus fruit), a combination of nature festival and religious procession, the waving of the *lulav* toward all corners of the universe, the prayerful procession around the pulpit, to prove the existence of a memory of the times when Jews were an agricultural and pastoral people. Even the sorrowful prayer for dew is a remnant of the days when the life of the Jew—his very bread—was dependent on the rain.

We know that the leaders of the Jewish communities, the

rabbis, prohibited dancing in public, and even within the home and synagogue too much joyous dancing was not permitted. This was true possibly as a result of the fear of the Gentiles among whom the Jews had to live, because of the permanent feelings of mourning which pervaded the Jewish life in the Diaspora, or because of the constant necessity to plead with the authorities for the smallest rights. Frequent persecutions and pogroms also stamped Jewish life with permanent sadness.

Nevertheless, there is no doubt that dancing never ceased entirely for the Jewish people especially among the women. In talmudic times there was a proverb to the effect that a woman is attracted to the sound of music like a six-year-old girl. The dance simply evolved into other forms. Holders of narrow religious views attempted to root out the *joie de vivre* which every Jewish woman guarded in her heart as the healthy inheritance of a happy people. We find proverbs which tell us that it is an abomination to listen to a woman sing. The attitude toward non-Jewish music was similar. This was true especially of the Greek songs, because everything of Greek origin was anathema to the talmudists who forbade the worship of the human body, and therefore the songs accompanying some of the Greek religious ceremonies.

Jews were permitted to sing sailor songs, sea chanties, and agricultural songs since at the beginning of the Middle Ages some Jews were still employed in these fields and such songs were an expression of their daily lives. During holidays the songs sung mostly dealt with God's grace and used melodies reminiscent of ancient religious rituals—the genuflections and bowings, the priestly blessings, the palm leaf and citrus ceremonies, and the *Hakafot* (processions with the Torah).

Since it was a *mitzvah* (good deed) to be happy at a wedding, wedding dances were permitted to conform with a tradition formed during talmudic times. Rabbi Yehuda was in the habit of dancing with a palm branch and singing, "Beautiful, pious bride," glorifying the woman in marriage.

Later, during the Middle Ages, Purim carnivals became very popular among the Jews. Purim plays and dramatic representations of Esther stories date from the tenth century. Jewish children in Italy formed groups which went about on horses. They blew trumpets, set up an effigy of Haman, and subsequently burned it in the course of a big parade.

In the fourteenth century the French and German Jews arranged masquerades presenting the Purim story accompanied by dancing and fireworks. The Purim masquerades and plays took definite form in the eighteenth century. In addition there were plays enacting the sale of Joseph in which the actors were *yeshivah* students.

After the twelfth century, just as each Jewish community had a communal kitchen for wedding festivities and a ritual bath, each community also possessed a dance hall. Dance was a purposeful part of Jewish social life. Mixed dancing probably crept into these dance halls, even though the rabbis fought against the idea of men and women dancing together.

It is necessary to note another important point regarding the Jews of Italy, Germany, and Poland. This concerns the role of the actor, or meistersinger. This was a sort of comedian, musician, and bear trainer. Many of them were also acrobats—they did tightrope walking and their wives and children danced. They were generally able to play the violin, harp, and flute.[2]

Because of the many plagues and pogroms, and the expulsion of Jewish communities from place to place, the number of vagabonds increased. From among these there developed various poets, entertainers, artists, and acrobats. At the same time there developed a group of minstrels, storytellers, and wandering *yeshivah* students. During the vagabonds' most fruitful epoch two dances became popular—the "Beggars' Dance" and the "Dance of Death." The "Beggars' Dance" was presented at weddings and fairs; the "Dance of Death" was presented at the cemetery. During the course of an epidemic, a poor couple would be chosen and married at the cemetery, and the "Dance of Death" would then be danced. The whole cemetery would become part of this type of wedding.

Jewish dancing in the Middle Ages was intimate, told a story, and had a lyric quality rather than the biblical pathos of earlier generations. The movements had tragic character. The dance was symbolic and filled with allusions containing a universal quality. It was not provincial or local and was different in each ghetto. The Middle Ages failed to provincialize the Jewish dance—they were merely responsible for the loss of strength which existed in biblical times. The universal quality of Jewish life and dance remained because of the constant wandering from country to country.

This article is reprinted from the Yidischer Cultur, *February, 1940, translated from the Yiddish by Albert Sheldon, American Zionist Council.*

---

[1] In Nathan Visonsky's book *Jewish Folk Dance* we read: "The dance is given a unique form of expression in the Yom Kippur dance as recorded in our Sacred Writings, wherein the young men of Israel watched the lovely maidens as they danced and chose their brides from among them. Girls would gather at an appointed place, all dressed in white and their robes similar to each other so that the poorest among them would not be ashamed, while the young men would stand some distance away in a group, eagerly watching their graceful steps and lithe bodies in motion. Sometimes during the dance a young man would approach and take a girl by the hand as a sign that she had found favor in his eyes. It is easy to see that such a dance was not simply calculated to amuse and entertain but was a matter of great importance in the life of the daughters of Israel. No silver loving cup was the prize of this dance contest but the blessing of marriage for the fortunate dancer."

[2] In Kurt Sachs's *World History of the Dance*, we find that " . . . the only dance master of whom we hear in the Middle Ages was a Jew, Rabbi Hacen ben Salomo, who, in the year 1313, in the Church of St. Bartholomew, at Tauste in the Spanish province of Zaragoza, had to teach the Christians to perform a choral dance around the altar." And in the fifteenth century, at the court of Urbino, a Jewish dancer, Guglielmo Ebreo of Pesaro, "excelled all men in the dance."

2 Treasure out of Yemen

SARA LEVI-TANAI

Sara Levi-Tanai, founder and director of Inbal, is a dedicated as well as singularly gifted woman. Israeli-born, of Yemenite parentage, she conceived the idea of preserving this rich vein of Yemenite tradition and molding it into an art form, and against great obstacles—one of these the strong objection of religious parents to their children's performing on a stage—she organized, trained, and developed Inbal. She is a teacher, choreographer, and musical arranger. Starting with a central theme, she works out the dance sequence, writes words of the songs, or adapts them from the Bible or the works of modern Hebrew writers. Traditional melodies, often out of the memories of members of the group, are used. In addition to her other talents, she is a noted composer.

In 1950 a group of young men and women of Yemenite origin met in a small hall in north Tel Aviv. They themselves weren't clear about what they wanted. Should they restrict themselves to Yemenite folklore or should they be an Israeli group made up of members of Oriental background?

One thing was certain: There was a great longing for expression. The Yemenite Jews have a rich store of experience and folklore and there was no need to go looking for material. We began to sing and to dance. But even from the beginning it was clear to us that our Yemenite sources alone would not be sufficient. Our aim was the creation of a permanent professional group and not the occasional union of people who are preparing one or two programs. What course then should we take?

The story of the development of Inbal cannot be told in a few words. Our ideas became clearer to us as we worked.

Little by little, step after step, the project developed, the repertory grew, and now three currents can be distinguished in the work of the company:

1. The Yemenite current, based upon the tradition and folklore of the Yemenites. This trend also includes free, modern creations based upon original songs and stylized Yemenite movement.

2. The biblical current, freely shaped works on subjects taken from the Bible. Here, also, the movement is chiefly Yemenite, but it is augmented by a tendency to broaden and enrich the movement and to make it express the drama.

3. The Israeli current. The spiritual tension in the building of the new Israel naturally influences every Israeli artist who shares the life of his nation. The feeling for the old-new landscape, the joy of redeeming the land and the desert, and the struggle for existence—all these supply a rich mass of material.

In 1950 the whole project seemed a daring thing. The pupils had never studied dancing or acting. All came from religious families where the theater is synonymous with idleness or even profligacy. The teacher herself was not overburdened with artistic training. She had only directed performances given by amateurs in schools and in children's theaters. None of us had any conception of the dance as an art in its own right.

However, "the Lord watches over fools." Naive as we were, we sang the songs of Yemen and the new songs of Israel. We performed Yemenite dances and Israeli shepherd dances. Our very first appearances, with all their unripeness, caught the public interest, especially in the workers' settlements which felt that Inbal was near to them in spirit. After every appearance in some isolated settlement or large kibbutz the same cry was heard: "This is ours. We understand it." Here the young group found much encouragement.

Then through the America-Israel Cultural Foundation,

known at that time as the American Fund for Israel Institutions, came great help. Artists like Jerome Robbins and Anna Sokolow revealed an interest in the budding enterprise. Miss Sokolow visited Israel several times, trained the members of the group, and laid the foundation for organized and professional work. Her help continued for the most daring of all our dreams—an extensive tour in Europe and in the United States of America.

As a Jewish, Israeli, and Oriental group, Inbal draws from rich spiritual storehouses. The thousand-year-old culture of Israel, which has stood the test of torment and shame, supplies every artist participating in the life of his nation with innumerable topics. What is also important is the spiritual content stored in every subject, the fruit of an ancient, continuous culture. This makes the dramatic touch of the Jewish, biblical, or Israeli subject more poignant for we are imbued with the feeling of our ancient landscape. The figure of the modern Israeli farmer and fighter does not fall short of its precursors in the Bible for the modern Israeli has also sprung up faithful to our ancient sources.

As a Jewish ethnic group whose place of exile has remained the Orient, we have at our command folklore which has rich ancient and Oriental traits. It can be said of Inbal that the problem of what to do and what material to draw on does not even exist. The sources, the ˜material, the background, and the stimulus exist in a blinding and oppressive abundance. There is a feeling that the silence of generations has been broken and the song has burst forth.

When Yeshayahu, Yehuda, Shoshanah, or Margalit sing, one can hear in their voices the lamentation of the desert in its broad expanses of wasteland and the distress of the individual in the burning landscape of the Orient, the same intense and charming landscape which brought forth stormy prophets, stubborn farmers, and shepherds, the visionaries of one great, wide world in which the human species lives in brotherhood and the Lord of Justice is his Lord.

On such a spiritual basis, almost every dance receives a deep and symbolic meaning. Without cutting itself off from the roots of reality, this expression rises to exalted heights.

In the first eight years we have created about ten dance pieces which form the basis for the technique of Inbal. This is a treasure, and the movements have broadened during the years. Now it is also beginning to be crystalized. But the act of branching out involves no diminution of strength. Ceaselessly new movements penetrated by a generally Oriental influence are being added to the elements of the Yemenite dance, movement, and gesture. Yemen lies in the southern part of the Arabian peninsula, and it is near Africa and India; what wonder then that the influence of these nearby countries is felt in its song and dance?

In everyday work this wealth of movement develops freely according to the need of the dramatic expression. At first things are created without special consciousness, but in the course of work the movements are clarified. The strange and the artificial are discarded and only those movements akin to our spirit remain.

And so we find in the dances of Inbal the movements of the Jews in time of prayer, inspired dances, the influence of the Arab *debka*, developments of movements of the hands, head and neck, characteristic of the Oriental dance. There are also seated dances while most of the dances are danced with the knees a little flexed.

Lately we have tried to sort out our movements, to note them down, and to evaluate them according to a definite order. In this way we shall lay the foundation for our school. Until now it has not been possible to teach the Yemenite dance because it was danced through improvisation. Inbal is studying the fundamental movements and bringing them to the consciousness of the dancer. When the Yemenite dancer knows what he does with each movement he will be able to

teach them to young Israeli men and women who are not
Yemenites. In this process it is possible that Yemenite movement as it was known in Yemen, a little twisted and smacking
a little of the Diaspora, will be lost, but in time it will be
passed on with greater breadth, erectness, clarification, and
confidence and will create for us a new dance whose field of
growth will be the new Israel.

This article is reprinted from the fall, 1957, issue of Israel Life and
Letters, *copyright 1957, by the American-Israel Culture Foundation.*

---

3 The Chasidic Dance

DVORA LAPSON

Dvora Lapson, who has been pioneering in the Jewish dance for over twenty-five years as dancer, choreographer, educator, and author, is at present director of the Dance Education Department of the Jewish Education Committee of New York and is on the staff of the School of Education and Sacred Music of the Hebrew Union College-Jewish Institute of Religion. Miss Lapson has done extensive research in Jewish dance in various parts of the world where she also gave recitals of Jewish dance. The above article was written before World War II, after a period of research in a number of Jewish communities in Poland which had been destroyed by the Nazis.

Isadora Duncan was so deeply moved by chasidic lore that she was determined to go to Palestine to study the ecstatic chasidic dance. As a matter of fact, Isadora was choosing the wrong country. Although numerous small communities of Chasidim were established in Palestine, the actual fountainhead of this unique social-religious revival movement was Poland and Eastern Europe.

So much of the ideology of the dancing Chasidim is similar to that of Isadora's, and even of our present-day dancers, that research into original sources proves a gratifying and rewarding activity. For Chasidism, unlike any other reform movement known to us, has made dancing a part of life, of the everyday life of millions of Jewish people. The chasidic dance was not composed deliberately nor did it originate as a folk dance. It arose as a conscious attempt to create human joyousness out of misery. Israel Baal Shem Tov, who, about 1736, emerged from the forests of the Carpathian Mountains where he spent many years as a recluse, was the young mystic

15

who inspired this reform. Millions of Eastern and Central European Jews were then leading a hopeless existence within the confines of the dreary and sordid ghetto. Chained in by medieval restrictions and limitations from the outside, the Jews were also oppressed by the rigid communal life which served as a sort of reaction to the outside world. The talmudists and rabbis of the ghetto, in their determination to save Israel from the spiritual onslaughts of the aggressive, hostile world, resorted to a literal interpretation of many precepts and commands in the Bible and required a blind observance of the minutiae of a rigorous and elaborate ritual. The life of the masses therefore became drab, miserable, colorless, and hopeless. The appearance of Baal Shem was a revelation. He taught that prayer performed with fervor and joy brought an instant realization of the nearness of God. He called for *prayer accompanied by physical ecstasy, dancing, and singing*. Immediately disciples sprang up. Wherever Chasidism penetrated, it brought a virtual revolution in the life of its followers. A new optimism pervaded the ghetto. Formal, dry worship made way for a new ritual which included dancing and melody.

The practice of preceding religious worship with dancing soon became the rule rather than the exception. Dancing figured so prominently in the new liturgy that it became indispensable to every gathering, whether religious or secular. Thanks to the new practices brought about by Chasidism, the physique of the Jew, shrunken and cramped as a result of generations of ghetto life, became more robust and normal. Wide and free gestures, essential in producing the desired expression of joyousness and exaltation replaced those of the cringing type.

The chasidic dance usually follows the tempo of chasidic music. Often, however, the dance proceeds independently with semi-improvised melody merely accompanying. Generally, the dance begins slowly with a touch of sadness expressive of yearning and mystery. It gradually assumes a faster rhythm until it reaches a state of ecstasy. The movements are basically the characteristic ghetto gestures and motions. At first, the forearm is used in quick, choppy movements from the elbow out. This is the most classic of all so-called Jewish gestures that have originated in the ghetto. As the Chasid warms up to his dance, with his feet raising him high in quick, jerky jumps and leaps, the arms, from finger to shoulder, begin to function very freely in expressive movements. His elbows, which cling close to his shrunken body in his daily life, are suddenly released and his arms are stretched upward in dramatic, meaningful gesticulations while his usually lowered head is raised and thrown back.

The great-grandson of the founder of Chasidism, Rabbi Nachman of Bratzlov (1772-1811), taught his followers that every part of the body had a rhythm of its own, that "there is a special rhythm in the movement of the whole body which corresponds to the rhythm of the melody." He believed that "as melody brought out the beauty in poetry, the dance brought it to a climax."

Despite the ravaging influence of the more modern period, with its mass emigrations, invasions of industrialism, and European culture, there are still many vestiges of the great chasidic realm in Europe where multitudes still permit their lives to be colored with a blissfulness that seems utterly incompatible with their present-day plight of economic privation. The chasidic dance is still holding its own. There is at present, for instance, one chasidic rebbe (Rabbi Halberstrom, officiating in Boboff, southern Poland) who has accustomed his followers to expect a new dance and melody from him every few weeks.

While the chasidic dance developed as an integral part of the new religious ritual, it is never entirely limited to the synagogue. The Chasidim have adapted their dances to every occasion of assemblage that offers an emotional outlet. There are special dances for the Sabbath feast when the rebbe (chasidic leader and teacher) and his followers welcome Queen Sabbath. These dances are danced around the banquet table and are always joyous and exalting. On the other hand, the dances of Shalosh Seudot, which are danced at twilight the next day at the hour marking the departure of Queen Sabbath and the approach of the days of toil and trouble, are permeated with mysticism and melancholy. There are special dances to commemorate the anniversary of the death of a *tzadik* (saint) or rebbe. This is contrary, incidentally, to the custom of non-chasidic Jews who consider such occasions wholly inappropriate for the expression of anything akin to joy.

Dancing at Jewish weddings has been traditional since ancient times. But, even here, the Chasid has made his contribution by introducing the spontaneous, unpremeditated, and spellbinding rhythm of his new dance. Although Chasidism has produced hundreds of dances that fit every occasion in the social and religious life of its adherents, it is claimed that never has a vulgar gesture or movement been introduced into a single one of its dances even when performed by the humblest and most uncultured members of the sect.

Today, one can still see many examples of the chasidic dances as practiced by the last remnants of the cult. In Palestine, several years ago, I had the opportunity to observe Chasidim, small groups of elderly people, dance with great abandon at the grave of the saint Rabbi Simeon Bar Yochai (reputed father of the Kabalah) at Meron in the hills of Galilee. Thousands upon thousands gathered and danced all night around the enormous fire that was lit near the holy tomb.

In Poland, where there are still about one million [1937] adherents of the cult, the Chasidim are divided into two major groups whose distinguishing features are reflected largely in their styles of dancing. The Chasidim of Warsaw and the surrounding country are known as the rationalists whose dance has developed a sense of esthetics without sacrificing any of the fervor. Their dance is refined, usually pensive in mood. In the province of Galicia, in southern Poland, however, Chasidism still boasts a good deal of its old glory, and its dances are characterized by great vigor, freedom, and abandon. Many of the rebbes of this province have attained wide reputations because of their original fervent dances and melodies. Most often the Chasidim dance around in circles, holding on to each other's shoulders or belts as they follow each other around. The rebbe is never hidden or "lost" among the dancers, always exercising the lead by his solo performance as well as directing by means of gestures and voice modulations. If the room is too small, a circle is formed within a circle, and the "whole house" dances joyously.

I visited the Rebbe of Tarnov, Galicia, during the Festival of the Rejoicing of the Law. I shall never forget his rapturous dance as he lifted the diminutive Torah scroll he had inherited from several generations of saintly forebears. The Chasidim stood around in a circle, singing a specific traditional melody and clapping their hands. Their faces seemed spellbound as their eyes were glued to the figure of the rebbe dancing in the center, lifting and lowering the little Torah and waving it in all directions in the manner of the ritual palm branch (lulav) at the Feast of Tabernacles. Passing the Torah on to one of his Chasidim, he covered his eyes with a silver-trimmed shawl and danced with great abandon to a melody which became faster and more exciting. His steps were light as he hopped and skipped from one side to the other, his hands placed on his wide belt. When he was almost prostrated, he stopped for a rest and motioned to the Chasidim to continue to dance in a circle until he was ready to start again.

Quite different was the Simchat Torah dance of the Melitzer Rebbe, also of Galicia. With his eyes closed and his face glowing with ecstasy, he led the joyous dance procession of the Torah. The procession slowed down many times as the rebbe danced four steps forward, four steps back, swaying the tremendous scroll from right to left as if it were as light as a prayer book. Wide-eyed Chasidim followed with their Torahs in simple steps and bending of knees to the rhythm of the music. Following the replacing of the Torahs in the ark, the rebbe embraced his nearest disciple in a dance of joy. They were joined by another and another, swinging around with quick steps. Among them was an old man of over one hundred years. With halting steps and hands held high, he followed his rebbe, proud to be so close to him. When steps failed him, he followed with his eyes. The Melitzer led the group around in a circle until the excitement reached a high pitch. Then he made his way to the center of the circle and danced by himself, improvising a myriad of beautiful movements with his arms, legs, and body.

In America, where thousands of European Chasidim made their new home, many chasidic centers, or *shtieblach*, have been established for the practice of some vestiges of this cult. But the youth has almost completely forsaken these practices in favor of more "worldly" ways. Thus Chasidism has loosened its hold on those whom it might have counted as its American followers. What will remain of it in this country is therefore difficult to say. The chasidic dance, however, has already found expression in the compositions of a number of contemporary concert dancers. The philosophy of Chasidism, based on the inherent nature of man to use rhythmic movement for emotional expression, deserves respect and admiration from the dance world.

This article is reprinted from the Dance Observer, *November, 1937.*

---

4 Jewish Dance Activities in America

FRED BERK

Fred Berk received his dance training in Europe and as a dancer toured America, Canada, Europe, and Israel.

He is founder and director of the Jewish Dance Division at the 92nd Street YM-YWHA in New York City. He was co-founder of the Merry-Go-Rounders dance company and then headed the Stage for Dancers project for five years producing and directing modern dance concerts at the Brooklyn Museum. In 1968 Mr. Berk was appointed director of the Israel folk dance department of the Zionist Youth Foundation. Many Israeli folk dance records have been issued under his supervision. In 1972, he joined the faculty of Gratz College, Philadelphia.

Jewish dance activities in America have been stimulated by the history and experiences of the Jewish people.

The strongest influence on these activities was the chasidic dance, one of the two really authentic Jewish folk dance styles that can be traced. The second authentic Jewish dance movement was preserved by the Yemenites.

The Chasidim who emigrated to the United States brought with them dances that played a very important part in their ceremonial and even daily life. Anyone who has been fortunate enough to see the Chasidim dancing in the streets of the Williamsburg section of Brooklyn on Simchat Torah, or similar happy occasions, must have taken away with him a realization of the vital part that dancing plays in the life of the Chasid. As we shall see, these dances, through which the pious Chasidim sought for a joyous unity with the universe, have done much to enrich the American Jewish dance scene.

Other Eastern European Jews who were not members of

the chasidic sect also brought their dances with them during the great pre-World War I migration to America. These dances did not play as important a part in their lives as the wordless *nigun* (melody) did in the life of the Chasid. However, they were, and are still, performed at weddings and holidays, usually in family surroundings.

These dances of the non-chasidic Eastern European immigrants were not uniquely Jewish, based as they usually were on Russian, Polish, or similar folk dances. But they did, over the course of generations, acquire a specific Jewish character that made them stand apart from the originals upon which they were based.

These, together with influences which were to come much later from Israel, are the roots upon which American Jewish dance activities are based today. Whole segments of the American Jewish community, who had been unaware of the richness and depth of their heritage, obtained new understanding and appreciation for their culture when, in 1926, the Moscow Habimah visited New York with its production of *The Dybbuk*. The play, through its magnificent use of gesture and line, created a furore in the theatrical and dance world. It was the first time that chasidic movement and dance steps were successfully included in a play in order to emphasize its action. Their "Beggars' Dance" became a famous theater piece.

A second important event occurred shortly afterward when Maurice Schwartz, in his production of *Yoshe Kalb*, portrayed the rejuvenescence that Jewish spiritual life experienced with the advent of Chasidism. This play, too, was outstanding for its dancing which was choreographed by an American dancer, Lillian Shapero. Miss Shapero, who was a member of the first Martha Graham dance company, continued to be active in the Jewish theater and also gave her own dance concerts which included many dances on Jewish themes. She was, however, but one of several outstanding dancers and choreographers who began to appear on the Jewish American theatrical and concert dance scene.

Benjamin Zemach, who came to this country in the Habimah group, decided to remain in America. He choreographed many Jewish plays and effective pageants. He also had his own dance company which toured a great part of the country. Dvora Lapson won renown primarily as a concert dancer and lecturer. She presented her Jewish dances in many countries. Her experiences with the chasidic dance can be found in the preceding chapter of this book. Nathan Visonsky organized his own Jewish ballet company which functioned over a ten-year period. He choreographed many great spectacles in the larger cities of the United States and published a charming book entitled, *Jewish Folk Dances*, in which he recreated a number of the dances of Eastern Europe. Corinne Chochem directed her own dance group, Rikkud Ami, and published two books, *Palestine Dances* and *Jewish Holiday Dances*. Miss Chochem holds the distinction of being the first in America to record Jewish and Palestinian dances using arrangements by such outstanding composers as David Diamond, Darius Milhaud, Castelnuovo-Tedesco, etc.

Naomi Aleh-Leaf was the first born Palestinian to perform in America. Her dances were based on themes on the Bible and the land of Palestine. On the West Coast, Ruth Zahava was a very active interpreter and also published a book of her own, *Jewish Dances*.

The theatrical Jewish dance has continued to make considerable advances in the United States. A number of American dancers have composed works using biblical themes such as the stories of Jacob and Rachel, Ruth, Deborah, and the Exodus. Pearl Lang has developed a scene based on *The Dybbuk*. Pauline Koner has composed a dance, "Voice in the Wilderness," inspired by the words of the prophet Isaiah, while Sophie Maslow has choreographed a group work entitled "The Village I Knew," based on the stories of Sholom Aleichem. The dancer Hadassah has composed and performed solo and group works on biblical, chasidic, and Israeli themes.

The repertory of the dance team of Fibich and Berg is concerned exclusively with Jewish themes. The Merry-Go-Rounders dance company performs a ballet called *Holiday in Israel*, the Festival of the First Fruits, which I created for this company.

Whatever these, as well as other active artists in the Jewish dance field at that time, accomplished depended completely on their Jewish backgrounds, on their individual creative techniques, and on their abilities to perform their dances in an exciting way.

This, in brief, was the state of development of the Jewish dance in America when I arrived in 1940.

The folk dance movement was at that time in its infancy. Some dances, which the pioneers (or *chalutzim*) brought to Palestine from Europe, were being danced here while some Eastern European dances had been choreographed and were included in the repertory of Jewish and international folk dance circles.

I found the dances of the Zionist youth groups, incorporating the zest and "swing" of American square dancing, both unique and exciting. Upon investigation, I found that these dances had been choreographed by American dance leaders of these Zionist movements. The "Double Hora," the "Dundai," and the "Ari-Ara" are among the Jewish dances which had their origins in this country.

Shortly after the end of World War II, I spent a weekend on a training farm for young people preparing themselves to emigrate to Palestine. Also visiting the farm was a young Palestinian who taught a vibrant new circle dance, "Mayim." This was one of the first dances to be brought here from Palestine and it stimulated an enthusiastic wave of Palestinian or, as they were soon to be known, Israeli folk dances here.

Today, almost every Jewish center and "Y" recognizes the recreational and educational value of these dances and includes them in its programs. There is hardly a Jewish holiday now which is not celebrated with folk dancing. Israeli dances are favorites in international folk dance circles. New York City has an annual Israeli folk dance festival in which all Zionist youth groups participate. Many folk dance books have been published in which the dances have been recorded.

Israeli folk dance exerts a great influence in the Jewish educational field. It also found special popularity in the international folk dance circles of America.

Three different dance companies from Israel toured the United States—Batsheva, a modern dance orientated group, The Music Hall of Israel, stressing folk dance, and Inbal, the Yemenite dance theater. The last one especially left a lasting impression of Jewish dance on the American scene.

The past and present are an endless source of inspiration for artists in Israel and America in developing what is only the beginning of a new art form. The raw material must be shaped and molded into a final creation which can then truly be called "The Dance of the Jewish People."

5 Folk Dance in Israel

GURIT KADMAN

Gurit Kadman is one of the founders of Israeli folk dance. She organized the first folk dance teachers' training seminars and published the first folk dance manuals which were used in these seminars. She founded the Palestinian dance group which performed at the International Youth Festival in Prague, Czechoslovakia, in 1947. She introduced Israeli dancing in Europe, America, Canada, and Japan. She produced dance films of returning immigrants from Yemen, Morocco, Libya, India, Iraq, etc. Presently Gurit Kadman is coordinator and chief adviser to Ulpan courses around the country.

The pioneers (*chalutzim*), who founded the new villages—kibbutzim and other collective settlements—in Eretz Yisrael, brought with them cultural values from all the European countries, especially from Eastern and Central Europe, and among them songs and dances. Thus, it happened that "our" dances in the pioneering days were the Hora, stemming from Rumania, the Polka and Krakoviak from Poland, the Cherkessia and Kossatshok from Russia, the Lithuanian Polka, Scotch, etc. And the Hora, one of the countless different Horas existing in Rumania as in all the Balkan countries, became almost our national dance. What were the qualities which made the Hora the favorite among all those dances?

This village dance, one of the simplest among all the Rumanian Horas, came to our country with settlers from Rumania at the turn of the century. It fitted perfectly the pioneer character of those settlers and the social setup of the kibbutz especially. The tightly closed circle, with linked arms and hands on shoulders of the neighbors, was the exact expression of the close human relationship between all the members of the community; all of them with equal rights and equal value, regardless of sex or of dancing ability. Simple and energetic movements—stamping, jumping, and leg swinging; the main thing being to go on for hours and hours. They sing and dance, circling and abandoning themselves to the togetherness and the group movement; the enthusiasm rises almost to ecstasy quietening down for a time and rising again; some leave and others join in, but the circle, the closely knit chain, remains and goes on like a magic ring.

It must be stressed that in the course of years the original Rumanian Hora changed in Israel so much that it is not recognizable any more. The shoulder-chain was abandoned in favor of simple holding of hands, giving more freedom of movement. The energetic stamps and leg-swinging disappeared and made room for small, light, elastic steps, with accentuated body turns; all the movements are narrower and more restrained, in short, more Oriental.

The Krakoviak, for many years the most beloved dance in couples, also changed so extensively that it no longer resembles its Polish origin; of its long and complex tune only two parts remained, and nothing reminds you of the varied, complicated, and colorful figures of the Polish Krakoviak; here, it is danced simply and primitively—stephops forward and then turning in a kind of Polka step which is also reduced to utter simplicity. A complicated and refined dance became a simple peasants' dance.

In spite of all the changes and adaptations of those dances, the fact remains that they are primarily of foreign origin.

In the early spring of 1944 a small number of interested people met and started thinking seriously about our folk dances. They began looking around the country to find out what were the existent dances; they examined historical and traditional sources of Jewish dances and wondered how it was possible that the Jewish nation with one of the oldest traditions in the world should be lacking a folk dance tradition. And this is what they found out—There is ample proof in the Bible and the Talmud of vivid folk dancing in those olden times: victory dances (Miriam, Yiphta's daughter), religious dances (King David), dances for the nature and harvest festivals, the "Machanayim" or contra dances in spring, for the Festival of the First Fruits, vineyard festival in summer, water drawing festival in fall, etc. It was obvious that Jews were a dance loving, dance rich nation in biblical times. But how did they dance? Could we revive those dances? It turned out that of those ancient dances no testimonies whatsoever remained which could help us to understand, to reconstruct, to revive them.

But then, in 1944, the sources for Jewish dances seemed deplorably sparse and poor and did not offer anything to build upon. For us people who fervently wished to have dances of our own and in our lifetime, there was no choice; one had to create dances, and it happened starting in 1944. It was clear that this was against all the laws of development of folk culture the world over. How can one create purposely, that is, artificially, folk dances which usually grow slowly like trees out of deep roots! How is it possible to accelerate a process of hundreds of years into a few years? Only a miracle can bring this about. But, after all, the same is true for the rebirth of the Jewish nation in its ancient long lost homeland when immigrants from all over the world, unaccustomed to productive work, endeavored to build agriculture, industry, a state with a national culture and economy in contradiction to all the laws of historical and economical logic and tradition—a constant miracle was needed.

Accordingly the folk dance enthusiasts put their faith in the miracle and started with action.

The first undertaking was a gathering of folk dancers at Kibbutz Dalia in the hills of Ephraim in the summer of 1944. It was to be a display of the existing dances, and the few organizers went to work with many apprehensions. The world war was still raging, terrible news about the slaughter of Jews in Europe came trickling in—and we prepared for a dance gathering. In its organization we were helped by the music committee of all the kibbutzim, the cooperative settlements. It was a great success, exceeding all our expectations and showing clearly the interest and sympathy for these first steps towards an indigenous folk art of our own, which prevailed in the collective settlements, and the love for dance of our youth. Notwithstanding all the difficulties both in transportation and in the work situation, two hundred dancers from all over the country took part in the dance gathering for two days and nights, and the concluding evening show drew an audience of 3,500 to that tiny lonely spot up in the hills, lacking even a decent highway. The program contained three parts—One, dances customary all over the country, nearly all of them borrowed from other countries; second, a small number of indigenous dances, some new, like "Goren" and "Mayim" (the water dance), one traditional "Sherele," some influenced by the Yemenite style; the third part, the most impressive one, dances of other countries in colorful costumes, Russian, English, Czech, Scandinavian dances, etc.

As evidence of existing dances of our own, it was a testimony of poverty. But the event was the turning point, followed by a general awakening of dance enthusiasm in the communal settlements and by a period of feverish creation of dances. In the kibbutzim new dances grew like mushrooms after the rain. There was a growing eagerness to learn new dances. The teaching and spreading of these dances was organized; a new "profession" came into being—dance leaders, who taught mainly in collective settlements. In the spring of 1945 the Israel folk dance committee was founded and soon after affiliated to the Cultural Department of the Histadrut Workers' Organization.

The second folk dance festival in Dalia in the summer of

1947 was like a demonstration of the *Yishuv* (Jewish population) against oppression and in favor of its rising indigenous folk culture. Five-hundred dancers took part in the *kinus* (gathering) which lasted two days and nights, and at the concluding evening, for the public performance, 25,000 people came from all over the country in spite of the night curfew which the British Mandatory government at that time had imposed upon the country. The onlookers sat all through the night on the ploughed furrows (instead of benches), in the large natural amphitheater near Kibbutz Dalia, watching the performances on the open stage down in the *wadi* (valley). The program contained only Israeli dances—folk dances and festive holiday dances alternating, nearly all of them newly created, the fruits of three years of creation. The hope for a miracle had happened—the indigenous Israeli folk dance was born, its cradle being the collective settlements, the village, the kibbutz, and the moshav.

From then on the new dances spread to the towns and cities as well and conquered the youth, helped to integrate new immigrants in the life of the country, shaped the character of big celebrations like Independence Day, etc., and were also received enthusiastically by Jews all over the world who quickly took to them as a means of identification with the new Israeli culture.

It is a fact that most of the people who create our dances are or have been living in kibbutzim or are closely connected with kibbutz life; the same is true for many of the composers of the dance songs.

Therefore, our dances do not have a specific theme; they express the joy of life and of collective motion and the exuberance of youth.

The direct impact of landscape, earth, seasons, and contact with the very specific society of the collective village has led to the creation of these songs and dances.

We are still in the initial phase of this creation and we have to grapple with many problems. All the factors which go with the folk dance, such as musical accompaniment, costume, decorations—a matter of course in traditional folk dance everywhere—pose for us unending problems. Every nation has its specific musical instrument; every tiny village has its orchestra, its costume, its decoration, its dance—customs in an established traditional context.

We have to create it.

In June 1968, our sixth folk dance festival took place at Dalia, planned as a celebration in song and dance for the twentieth jubilee of the State of Israel.* This time 3,000 dancers took part and the amphitheater had seats for 30,000 onlookers. In two consecutive evenings of performances, the story of Israel's new settlements was performed in music and dance on five stages.

This was the biggest dance festival in Israel so far. But we are looking forward to a festival with international participation. We hope to have some day a "Mediterranean Festival" with all the surrounding countries celebrating with us in song and dance the much longed for peace.

---

*Previous folk dance festivals: in Dalia, 1944, 1947, 1951, 1958; and in Beth Berl, 1963.

Mitzvah dance

Dance of the entertainer

After the wedding

Pictures of a chasidic wedding. Courtesy Zvi Friedhaber, Haifa

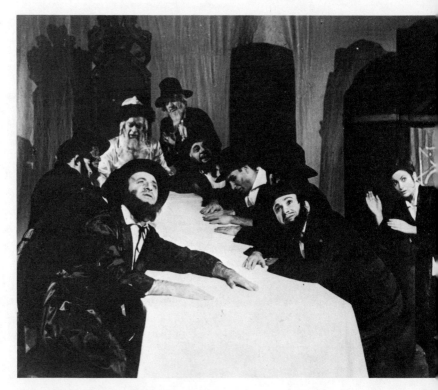

The famous Habimah theater in "The Dybbuk." A legend of chasidic life. Zionist Archives and Library

Dance pageant in Jerusalem. Zionist Archives and Library

"Hora." As danced by the youth of Ein Harod. Zionist Archives and Library

"Hora." Hebraica dancers. Photo, Fred Fehl

Christian Arab girls from East Jerusalem dancing a Lebanese Debka. Dalia festival, 1968. Government Press Office

Yemenite fathers and sons. Dalia festival, 1968. Government Press Office

Around the campfire. Zionist Archives and Library

Independence Day celebration. Dancing in the streets. Zionist Archives and Library

Dancing on a float. Israel Independence parade, 1969. Fifth Avenue, New York City. Altar Photographers

"Dance of the Harvesters." Dalia festival, 1944. Zionist Archives and Library

"Blessing of Wadi." Festival in a kibbutz. Zionist Archives and Library

Druz dancing in a village. Zionist Archives and Library

Yemenite men in a typical dance movement. Government Press Office

Three hundred and fifty dancers in finale of twentieth Israel folk dance festival at the Felt Forum in New York City, 1970. Photo, Louis Peres

PART II

Leader's Guide
to Israeli Folk Dances

1 Fundamentals of Folk Dancing

There are five basic elements which are necessary to know in order to be clear and specific about a dance: *Steps, Rhythm, Space, Dynamics, and Characteristics.*
Following are the definitions:

STEPS

1. *Walking* - shifting of weight from one foot to the other.
2. *Running* - fast shifting of weight.
3. *Leaping* - shifting of weight in the air, from one foot to the other.
4. *Jumping* - taking weight off the floor, lifting both feet simultaneously and landing on both.
5. *Hopping* - taking weight off from one foot and landing on the same.
6. *Skipping* - a combination of step-hop—it is not a basic step.

RHYTHM

Rhythm is the organized division of time.
To make the student more conscious of a rhythm, the teacher should clap it first and have the student repeat it. For example, if in a dance there are two slow steps and four fast ones, the student will have to clap slowly twice and fast four times. By so doing, it will be easier to transfer the rhythm to the feet.

SPACE

1. *Formation* - of couple dances, lines, squares, and circles. There are endless variations of space patterns which differ in

almost every dance. Their differences should be made very clear to the students.

2. *Direction* - of forward, backward, sideward right, sideward left. A circle is a combination of the four basic directions. Diagonals are between the basic directions. There are two levels, high (jumps and leaps) and low (squatting or on the floor).

Up to now, the first three basic elements were discussed. Every given instruction must include these three basic elements. For example:

Movement	Direction	Rhythm
1. step on right foot	2. forward	3. count 1

After the student learns the dance and knows it well, the last two elements should be introduced.

DYNAMICS

Dynamics is the strength or the accents in which a dance is performed. If such accents are not included, a dance will be dull and monotonous. Dynamics in dance relates to dynamics in music, in which various degrees of loudness and softness create the necessary expression.

CHARACTERISTICS

Once a pupil masters all the above-mentioned points, the teacher will have to explain the characteristics of a dance. These characteristics determine its style and execution. There are love dances, gay and flirtatious ones. A dance might have a bouncy quality like the Arabic dances or be fluid and soft like the dances of the Yemenites. They can be vigorous and ecstatic like most "Horas." These differences will influence the movement quality and the style of a dance.

With added dynamics and characteristics, the pupils will become emotionally involved. They will not only do mechanical steps and movements but will also experience the essence of folk dancing.

2 Teaching Beginners

When a teacher meets a group for the first time, it is most important that he makes the pupils feel completely at ease. They must feel very comfortable about the steps they are about to learn and be given the feeling that they will be able to execute them without difficulty. When teaching beginners, the simplest dance should be selected. This way, no one in the group will have difficulty following the teacher's instruction. An atmosphere of enjoyment and unity is thus immediately created.

An important point to emphasize is that "anyone who can walk can folk dance." Folk dancing is actually "walking to music," and this is what they should attempt to do. Psychologically, this definition helps people a great deal; they usually tend to become very tense when thinking in terms of "dancing." When told to walk, however, they will feel much more comfortable and more relaxed.

Another important aspect in teaching folk dancing is that beginners should not be bothered with details about movements and steps. On the contrary, the teacher should simplify the steps if necessary and not trouble them with burdensome and complicated details. If beginners are forced to do steps they cannot execute, they will feel stiff and very awkward and unable to enjoy it. They will probably never try to folk dance any more.

The main task in introducing the newcomers to folk dancing is to arouse the emotions of the participants and give them the feeling of accomplishment, of exhilaration, and of genuine fun.

3 Points for the Teacher

Be thoroughly prepared before facing a class. Know your material very well.

Tell the name of the dance. If possible, interpret the meaning. Then stress the formation. Which way to face—clockwise or counterclockwise, etc. Always start with feet together, with equal distribution of weight on both feet. This way one can start with the right or left foot.

Do not teach a Yemenite step to beginners. It is difficult. If you have to, modify the step until your pupils are ready. Then teach it the proper way.

Teach every dance in sections. Repeat each section until the group remembers it well. Only then should you continue with the next part. To remember movements and steps is a new experience for beginners. Therefore, it is necessary to teach a dance in a gradual development.

If you feel a dance cannot be taught successfully in a circle, let the pupils form lines facing forward. You will have to stand with your back to your pupils in order to face the same way. After you are confident that your pupils have learned the steps, they can return to do the dance in the proper formation.

Use images to get movement qualities across. For example a shuffling step can be taught by having your pupils pretend that they are walking on sand and creating a swishing sound. Or jumping in place can be accomplished much better if the students are told that the floor is burning hot and they cannot stop on the floor but must try to stop in the air.

Prompt steps in order to facilitate the learning process of a dance. Stop prompting only when you are sure that everyone remembers the sequence.

You have to be patient. You must never lose your temper.

You must make students understand that with practice the most difficult hurdle can be overcome.

You should give encouragement wherever you feel it is necessary.

You should be able to project to your students your enthusiasm about the material you are teaching.

A teacher has to have empathy, he should understand the problems a student has to go through while learning a dance. Then he will not just be a teacher but a very good one.

4 Folk Dance Choreography

Folk dance is enjoyable only for those who participate. Therefore, one must make changes if one wants to present such dances to an audience.

By folk dance choreography we mean arranging of a dance or the theme and variation form. One takes an existing dance and by changing its elements makes it varied enough for a presentation.

The choreography should present the theme for the dance in its original form, at least, once; after that, he is free to use many aspects which make a dance more theatrical: change of formation, rearranging of steps, emphasis on dynamics, variation of rhythm, use of props, and narration.

Sometimes the theatrical effect can be achieved by using only one of the above-mentioned elements. The basic form and spirit of a dance should be kept intact. If it is a circle dance, the succeeding variations should be round. The same thing applies for line and couple dances.

Entrances and exits for the group should be made a part of the presentation because most of the time folk dances are performed without a stage. Even if there is a professional stage, do not use, for example, pretentious lighting effects. One must not forget that the dancers are amateurs, but one can achieve wonderful results with such a group if one is able to arouse their spirit and joy of dancing. Without these two elements a folk dance will not serve the purpose of a performance.

Never force dancers into steps or movements they cannot learn easily. Even if there is only one person in a group who cannot execute a step as well as the others, the leader should simplify the movement for the entire group to unify their level.

A choreographer must never neglect the precision of a group. This means work and a lot of rehearsing. The mood and characteristic of a dance or scene should be stressed at all times, if the group is to become emotionally involved in the dance.

These are some of the tools one can work with in order to achieve a successful folk dance performance.

5 How to Start a Folk Dance Group

When I meet people on my travels throughout the United States, the question I most often hear from folk dance enthusiasts is *"How can I start an Israeli folk dance group in our community when there is no apparent interest in folk dancing?"* Personally I do not believe in this argument because if the right person undertakes such a project it will be successful. This person must have the desire to share the joy of folk dancing with others, the skill of an excellent teacher, and a terrific, limitless drive.

To secure sponsorship for such an activity is a very important first step. One has to contact community centers, temples, or local "Y's." If the idea is properly presented to a director of any of these or other organizations, it should not be too difficult to find a place to hold the dance sessions. Today, every educator in the field of Jewish culture or Jewish communal services accepts Israeli folk dancing as an important educational, social, and physical activity widely engaged in. They are also aware that such classes will not only attract Jews of all ages but people from a diversity of backgrounds, religions, and races.

Here are two approaches which will insure a successful beginning for any group:

1. Collect the names of friends who might serve as the nucleus of such a group. In the beginning one should be certain of having at least six to eight students before even sending out announcements or making up flyers.

2. Inviting a well-known personality in the profession for a guest workshop session will help attract people. At this session one can announce the formation of a weekly group.

People can sign up then and there. Of course, having a budget with provisions for inviting guest instructors is helpful.

Hopefully, a few more than merely the nucleus group will show up for the first session. To insure further success for the embryonic group, a good public relations job is extremely important. Concentrated efforts should be made to start a mailing list or to augment one already in existence. Supervision of mass mailings, stenciling of flyers, drawing posters, etc., should be the job of the responsible group leader or instructor. As personal contact is of the utmost importance, he should also make phone calls to Jewish organizations, international folk dance groups, physical education departments of colleges, yeshivahs, public high schools, etc., to have new activities and programs announced and publicized, thus attracting a larger audience or attendance. The best public relations job is done by word of mouth. If people enjoy the folk dance classes they will bring their friends.

It is a good idea to have the introductory session or class centered around the theme of a holiday, such as Chanukah, Purim, or Israel Independence Day. It is of the utmost importance that the right material be selected for such a session. Very simple dances should be chosen, such as "Vedavid," "Zemer Atik," "Hora Medura," "Mayim," etc. With dances such as these the teacher can instill in the participants the sense of accomplishment found in folk dancing.

A first session might not always be successful; therefore, it should be tried again and again. But, if after a few weeks a small group of regulars has been established, attempts can be made to demonstrate a few new dances at different meetings in order to recruit new members. Being a dance leader and organizer of a successful group can turn into a frustrating experience at times, but, when one succeeds, the sense of accomplishment and satisfaction will more than make up for the trouble.

6 Suggestions for Costumes

For a performing group, costumes are necessary. Since there is not yet a standard Israeli national costume, each dance leader will have to design the costumes for his group. However, there are national colors: blue and white. These colors can be used for a basic costume:

1. *Girls* - white peasant blouses and blue wide skirts (no mini skirts). Or white blouses and white skirts with blue sashes.
2. *Boys* - blue pants and white dress shirts. Or white pants and white shirts with blue sashes.

If girls are skillful enough to sew their own dresses, another combination can be used—blue dresses with white trimmings.

Boys can appear in white with blue trimming.

Examples of Israeli dance costumes

7 Catalog of Israel Folk Dance Records

English transliterations of names of dances are copied from the labels of the records.

These dances are numbered according to their level: Children (1), Beginners (2), Intermediate (3), Advanced (4).

Each album includes instructions unless indicated.

This catalog is offered by the Israel Folk Dance Department of the American Zionist Youth Foundation.

ISRAEL (FOLK DANCES)   Label: Israel LP 7
Conducted by Ne'eman-Elyakum with Theodore Bikel, Rachel Hadass, Martha Schlamme, Mort Freeman. Dance consultant: Dvora Lapson

Side One:
   Le'or Chiyuchech (3)
   Mehol Hanoar (3)
   Bat Yiftach (3)
   Hana'ava Babanot (4)
   Sherele (3)

Side Two:
   Mezarei Yisrael (3)
   Vehaya K'etz Shatul (1)
   Bat Harim (2)
   Mechol Hagat (1)
   Tcherkessia (1)

HORA   Label: Elektra LP 186
With the Oranim Zabar Troup. Soloist, Geula Gill. Arrangements by Dov Seltzer. Dance supervision: Fred Berk
                              (no instruction)

Side One: Side Two:
  Mayim (1)   Hora Mechona (1)
  Hine Ma Tov (2)   Dodi Li (3)
  Im Hashachar (1 & 4)   Bat Hareem (2)
  Harmonica (2)   Mechol Ovadya (2)
  Iti Milvanon (3)   El Ginat Egoz (3)
  Krakowiak (3)   Vedavid (1)

ISRAEL (FOLK DANCES)   Label: LP 5/6
Conducted by Elyakum Shapiro with Martha Schlamme and
Mort Freeman. Dance consultant: Dvora Lapson

Side One: Side Two:
  Mayim (1)   Ken Yovdu (3)
  Hanoded (2)   Lech Lamidbar (3)
  Hora Agadati (3)   Bo Dodi (2)
  Im Hoopalnu (3)   Sovevuni (3)
  Malu Asamenu Bar (3)   Hava Netze B'mahol (3)

FOLKDANCES OF ISRAEL   Label: Menorah 204
Music arranged by Dov Seltzer. Singer, Geula Gill. Dance
consultant: Rivka Sturman   (no instruction)

Side One: Side Two:
  Kol Dodi (3)   Ve'david (1)
  Hine Matov (2)   Zemerlach (2)
  Ahavat Hadassah (3)   Kuma Echa (1)
  Dodi Tsach Ve'adom (2)   Im Ba'arazim (3)
  Be'er Basadeh (3)   Hava Netze B'machol (3)
  Or Chavatsalot (2)   Megadim Le'er'l (3)

DANCE ALONG WITH SABRAS   Label: Tikva LP 69
Arrangements by Ami Gilad. Dance supervision: Fred Berk

Side One:
  Hava Netze (3)
  Hanokdim (4)
  Hora Neurim (3)
  Taam Haman (3)
  Ez Vakeves (4)
  Horat Hasor (3)
  Debkat Habir (4)

Side Two:
  Al Tira (4)
  Likrat Shabat (3)
  Haroa Haktana (4)
  Mechol Halahat (4)
  Roe Vero'a (3)
  Hora Mamtera (4)
  Hora—Hava Nagila (1)

ISRAELI FOLK DANCE FESTIVAL   Label: Tikva LP 80
Arrangements by Ami Gilad with Geula Zohar. Dance supervision: Fred Berk

Side One:
  Dayagim (4)
  At Va'ani (2)
  Kod Dodi (3)
  Al Tiruni (4)
  Ei Hatal (4)
  Yesh Et La'amol (3)

Side Two:
  Bat Arad (4)
  Ki Tinam (4)
  Debka Gilboa (4)
  Nad Ilan (3)
  Eretz Zavat Chalav (3)
  Debka Rafiach (4)
  Scotch (3)

DANCE WITH RIVKA   Label: Tikva 98
Music arranged and directed by Shai Burstyn. Dance consultant: Rivka Sturman

Side One: Side Two:
  Erev Ba (3)   Hashual
  Lean Noshevet Haruach   Hava Netz B'machol (3)
  Syn-Co-Pe   Israeli Mixer
  Israeli Mazurka (3)   Debka Leadama (4)
  Hora Simkat He'amel (3)   Ani Ledodi
  Jonati   Ne'arez B'hol Mishlat

FOLK DANCE IN ISRAEL TODAY   Collectors Guil CG-638
Israeli and European folk dances. Music played by Effy
Netzer. Singer, Regina Zarai
                          (no instruction)

Side One: Side Two:
  Kuma Aha (1 & 2)   Horah N'urim (3)
  Hineh Ma Tov (2)   Mazurka (3)
  Nigun Atik (2)   Ez Vakevez (4)
  Horah Nirkoda (2)   Erev Ba (3)
  Bat Hacarmel (3)   Debka Halel (4)
  Alexandrovah (3)   Korovushkah
  Cherkessia K'fulah (2)   Hamahol Hay'vani
  Merkavah   Krakoviyak (3)

DEBKA   Label: Tikva LP 100
Arrangements by Ami Gilad. Dance supervision: Fred Berk

Side One: Side Two:
  Debka Halel (4)   Zemir Atik (1)
  Debka Debka (4)   Ma Navu (2)
  Debka Daluna (4)   Hora Nirkoda (2)
  Hein Yerunan (4)   Kalu Raglayim (3)
  Debka Dayagim (4)   Eten Bamidbar (4)
  Debka Druz (4)   Niguno Shel Yossi (2)

DANCE FOR FUN   Label: Tikva 104
Music arranged and conducted by Shai Burstyn. Singer, Geula
Zohar. Dance consultant: Ayalah Goren

Side One: Side Two:
  Mi Yivne Bayit (3)   Hora Eylat (4)
  Hamekholelet (3)   Et Dodim Kala (4)
  Bona Habanot (2)   Uvanu Batim (4)
  Debka Kn'an (4)   Rikud Hakad (4)
  Ka'agadat Rivka (4)   Debka Hakatsir (4)
  Nitsaney Shalom (3)   Debka Hakhamor (4)
  Hoppa Hey (3)

SOUVENIR FROM ISRAEL   Label: Tikva 148
Music arranged by Shai Burstyn. Dance consultant:
Fred Berk

Side One: Side Two:
  Tslil Zugim (2)   Yarad Dodi Legano (2)
  Bein N'Har Prat (3)   Hora Chemed (4)
  Pashtu Kvasim (3)   Lamnatseach (3)
  Gozi Li (4)   Harimon (3)
  Mitsva Tanz (2)   Tzadik Katamar (2)
  Mish'al (4)   Ronee Bat Tsion (2)

DANCES FOR CHILDREN   Label: Tikva 106
Music arranged and directed by Shai Burstyn. Singer, Ahuva
Zadok. Dance consultant: Fred Berk

Side One: Side Two:
  Hora Medley (1)   Hora Medura (1)
  Simi Yadech (1)   Havu Lanu Yayin (1)
  El Harahat (1)   Mechol Hagat (1)
  Kuma Echa (1)   Patch Dance (1)
  Tcherkessia (1)   Mayim (1)
  Yemina, Yemina (1)   Shibolet Basadeh (1)
  Vedavid Yefei Eynayim (1)   Vehaya Ke'Eitz Shatul (1)

POTPOURRI   Label: Tikva 117
Music arranged by Ami Gilad. Dance consultant: Fred Berk

Side One: Side Two:
  Machar (3)   Hacormim (3)
  Shiru Hashir (4)   Debka Dalia (4)
  Bat Hacarmel (3)   Bat Tsurim (2)
  Debka Kurdit (4)   Mi Yitneini Ohf (3)
  Ana Halach Dodech (3)   Vaynikehu (3)
  Frelach (2)   Inbalim (3)
  Keshoshana (3)

ISRAELI FOLK DANCES   Label: Hadarim LP 1
Presented by the Hadarim. Musical arrangements by Eldad
Peery. Dance supervision: Shlomo Bachar
                                    (no instruction)

Side One: Side Two:
  Hashachar (4)   Erev Shel Shoshanim (3)
  Hoppa Hey (3)   Lean Noshevet Haruach (3)
  Erev Ba (3)   Bat Yiftach (3)
  Larokdim Heidad,   Debka Rafiach (4)
    Hora Medura (1)   Shibolet Basadeh (1)
  Ma Navu (2)   Hora Eylat (4)

PANORAMA   Label: Tikva 140
Musical arrangements by Ami Gilad. Dance supervision: Fred
Berk

Side One: Side Two:
  Shiboley Paz (3)   Hadoodaim (3)
  Nitzanim (4)   Uri Zion (2)
  Hora Bialik (2)   Vayiven Uziyahu (3)
  Tfillat Hashachar (4)   Adarim (3)
  Hagavia (4)   Hora Chassidit (2)
  Kumi Ori (3)   Te Ve'Orez (2)

RIKUDEY-AM   Label: Tikva 138
This record is recommended for the teacher. Music arranged
by Ami Gilad. Dance consultant: Fred Berk

Side One: Side Two:
   "Dances for children"   "Basic popular dances"
   Mechol Hagat (1)   Harmonica (2)
   El Harahat (1)   Zemer Atik (1-2)
   Shibolet Basadeh (1)   Mechol Ovadya (2)
   Patch Dance (1)   Vedavid (1-2)
   Hora Medura (1)   Kuma Echa (1-2)
   Yemina, Yemina (1)   Dodi-Li (3)
   Tcherkessia (1)   Hine Ma Tov (1-2)

NEW FOLKDANCES OF ISRAEL   Label: Tikva 142
Musical arrangements by Uri Hodorov. Dance supervision:
Moshe Eskayo

Side One: Side Two:
   Shiboley Paz (3)   Shetey Yonim
   Ha'eer Beafor   Simchu-Nu
   Hacormim (3)   Ma Avarech
   Befat Hakfar   Dror Yikra
   Debka Skayo   Salach
   Orcha Midbar (4)   Be'er Basadeh (3)

NA'ARAH   Label: I.F.C. 1
Musical arrangements by Shlomo Shai. Dance consultant:
Moshe Eskayo

Side One: Side Two:
  Na'arah   Debka B'not Hakfar
  Livavteenee (3)   Ad Or Haboker
  Debka Skayo   Al Gemali (3)
  Ma Avarech   Nitzanim
  Sapari (4)   Elem Ve'susato
  Uzi   Zemer Ikarim

ISRAELI FOLK DANCE PARTY   Label: Tikva 145
Musical arrangements by Shai Burstyn. Dance supervision:
Fred Berk

Side One: Side Two:
  Ki Hivshiloo (3)   Dror Yikra (4)
  Im Bearazim (2)   Yibanei Hamigdash (2)
  Mechol Hadvash (4)   Debka Bedouit (4)
  Bechazar Harabbi (1)   Shimu-Shimu (3)
  Kissufim (2)   Debka Chag (2)
  Rav Brachot (2)   Shuv Yotze Hazemer (3)

HOW TO ORDER

Records can be obtained through the Israel Folk Dance
Department, 515 Park Ave., New York, N.Y. 10022. Ask for
order blank.

---

8 Suggestions for Holiday Use

Key to the holidays.

A. Sabbath
B. Simchat Torah
C. Weddings
D. Passover

E. Independence Day
F. Chanukah
G. Tu Bi-Shevat (Arbor Day)

CIRCLE DANCES

Ma Navu (A)
Harmonica (B)
Mayim, Mayim (G)
Kuma Echa
Hora Medura (G)
At Va'Ani (C)

Al Tira (E)
Haroa Haktana
Mamtera (B)
Erev Ba
Lech, Lech Lamidbar (D)

COUPLE DANCES

Vedavid Yefe Eynaim
Zemer Atik (B + A)
Dayagim
Keschoshana Bein Hachochim

Dodi- Li (C)
Krakoviak
Ez Vakevez (D)
Bat Yiftach

LINE DANCES

Shiru Hashir (E)
Hine Ma Tov (A)
Debka Rafiach (E + F)

Debka Druz
Debkat Habir (E + F)
Debka Dayagim

The music of each dance can be found on the record as indicated under the title.

9 Terminology and Abbreviations

Before reconstructing a dance, carefully read the following explanations.

Step:	Put full weight on foot
Touch:	No weight on foot
R:	Right foot
L:	Left foot
Fwd:	Forward
Bwd:	Backward
Swd:	Sideward
CW:	Clockwise
CCW:	Counterclockwise

Most dances have a 4 measure introduction. All the steps described are done to 1/4 note unless otherwise indicated. Also every step can be reversed starting with the other foot.

Step-hop:	Step and hop on the same foot (2 counts)
Yem L:	Yemenite step left. L steps to left side (bend knee). R steps on toe behind L. L crosses in front of R. On 4th count pause.
Yem R:	Reverse Yemenite step left. Start with R.
Yemenite step fwd:	R fwd and bend right knee. L fwd on toe. R fwd. Pause.
Mayim step:	Face center of circle. L crosses in front of R. R steps to the right side. L crosses behind R. R to the right side.

Harmonica step:	L crosses in front of R. R bwd. L to left side. Hop on L.
Tcherkessia step:	R fwd. L bwd. R bwd. L fwd.
Double Tcherkessia step:	R crosses over L in front. L bwd. R to right side and reverse. (6 counts)
Waltz step:	R fwd and bend knee. L fwd on toe. R fwd on toe.
Mazurka step:	R fwd. L fwd. Hop on L.
Balance step or fast Yemenite:	R to right side. L in place. (1 count) Step on R in place. (2 counts)
Slow step:	One step to 2 counts.
Step bend:	Step fwd, or swd. Bend knee of the same foot. (2 counts)
Skating position:	Partners stand side by side. Girl on boy's right. His straight right arm and her bent right arm join hands in front of body. Her straight left and his bent left do the same. This position can also be done behind body.
Pivot:	Partners with right arms around each other's waist. Step on inside foot (bend knee). Step on outside foot on toe. Continue and turn CW, like the American "Swing Your Partner."

PART III

Twenty-Five Popular Israeli Folk Dances in America

1 Circle Dances

MA NAVU (How Pleasant) Dance: Raya Spivak
Music: Josef Spivak
Tikva LP 100

Formation: Circle, face center, all join hands

PART ONE
  1-2: R points fwd
  3-4: R points swd
  5: R bwd
  6: L closes to R
  7: R fwd
  8: Hold
  9-10: L bwd
11-12: R fwd
13: L bwd
14: R fwd
15: L closes to R
16: Hold
17-32: Reverse 1-16

PART TWO
  1-3: Yem R
  4: 1/4 turn on R to right side (face CCW)
  5-7: 3 steps fwd LRL
  8: 1/4 turn on L to left side (face center)
  9-32: Repeat 1-8 three more times

HARMONICA (Mouth organ)   Dance: Rivka Sturman
                               Music: Alconi
                               Tikva LP 138

Formation: Circle, join hands, face center of circle

PART ONE
  1-4:   Mayim step L
  5-6:   Face CCW. Step-hop L fwd
  7-8:   Step-hop R fwd
  9-32:   Repeat 1-8 three more times

PART TWO
  1-4:   Face center. Harmonica step L. Clap on first count, arms up high. On next 3 counts arms down
  5-8:   Harmonica step R
  9-12:   Repeat 1-4
13-14:   Face CW. Step-hop R fwd, arms crossed behind back
15-16:   Step-hop L fwd
17-32:   Reverse 1-16

PART THREE
  1-2:   Face center, arms on each other's shoulders. Step-hop L to left side
  3-4:   Step-hop R to right side
  5-8:   Face CW. 4 running steps fwd LRLR
  9-32:   Repeat 1-8 three more times

MAYIM, MAYIM (Water, Water) Dance: Folk
                                Music: Amiran
                                Tikva LP 106

Formation: Circle, all face center, all join hands, move CW

  1-16: 4 Mayim steps, start R
17-20: 4 steps fwd, start R. Raise arms
21-24: 4 steps bwd, start R. Lower arms
25-32: Repeat 17-24
33-36: Face CW, run 4 steps fwd, start R
37-44: Face center. Hop 8 times on R. On uneven counts
        point L fwd toward center. On even counts point L
        to left side
45-52: Release hands and reverse 37-44. Raise arms and clap
        on uneven counts 4 times

KUMA ECHA (Arise Brothers)

Dance: Rivka Sturman
Music: Postolsky
Tikva LP 138

Formation: Circle, face center, all join hands

PART ONE
1: R fwd
2: L fwd
3: R fwd
4: Hop on R
5-8: Reverse, start L bwd
9-12: Mayim step, R over L. Move CW
13-16: Repeat 9-12
17-32: Repeat 1-16

PART TWO
Face CCW
1: Run R fwd
2: Run L fwd and 1/2 turn to left side (face CW)
3: Run R bwd
4: Run L bwd and 1/2 turn to right side (face CCW)
5-16: Repeat 1-4 three more times
Face center
17-19: 3 running steps fwd RLR
20: Leap on L fwd
21-24: Tcherkessia R
25-32: 2 more Tcherkessia steps. On last 3 measures move
gradually back to original place

HORA MEDURA Dance: Yoav Ashriel
(Hora Around the Campfire) Music: Alterman
Tikva LP 138

Formation: Circle, face center, all join hands, move CCW

  1: R to right side
  2: L crosses behind R
  3-8: Repeat 1-2 three more times
  9-12: 4 steps fwd, start R
13-16: 4 steps bwd, start R
17-32: Repeat 1-16

Reverse direction, move CW
33-36: Mayim step R
37-40: Face CW. Run 4 steps fwd, start R. Body bends down
41-44: Face center. Mayim step R. Body up
45: Right heel touches the floor diagonally right fwd, arms
    up
46: Hold
47-48: Repeat 45-46
49-64: Repeat 33-48

AT VA'ANI (You and Me)   Dance: Danny Uziel
                                Music: Gilad
                                Tikva LP 80

Formation: Lines or circle, face center, join hands

PART ONE
1:      L to left side
2:      Hold
3:      R brushes in front of L
4:      Hold
5:      Bend left knee
6:      Stretch left knee
7:      Bend left knee
8:      Stretch left knee
9-16:   Reverse count 1-8
17-19: Yem L
20:     R to right side
21:     L crosses in front of R
22:     R to right side
23:     L crosses in front of R
24:     Hold
25:     R bwd
26:     L bwd
27:     R fwd
28:     Hold
29-32: Reverse 25-28
Music repeats, reverse count 1-32

PART TWO
1:      L to left side
2:      Hold
3:      R crosses in front of L, bend knees
4:      Hold

5-8: Repeat count 1-4
9: Release hands. L in place plus 1/2 turn to left side
10: Hold
11: R in place plus 1/2 turn in place to left side. With last 2 steps complete one full turn
12: Hold
13-16: Join hands. Yem L
17-32: Reverse 1-16

AL TIRA (Dance of Strength)

Dance: Jonathan Karmon
Music: Zeira
Tikva LP 69

Formation: Circle, face center, bend fwd, arms down

PART ONE
- 1: R to right side. Swing arms to right side
- 2: Hold
- 3: L to left side, swing arms to left side
- 4: Hold
- 5: Leap on R to right side
- 6: L crosses in front of R
- 7-8: Tap twice with right heel next to L
- 9: Face CCW. Lift body. Leap on R fwd
- 10: 2 running steps fwd LR
- 11: 2 running steps fwd LR
- 12: L fwd
- 13-16: Repeat 9-12
- 17-32: Repeat 1-16

PART TWO
- 1: Face center. Release hands. Step R in place
- 2: Hop on R. Kick L fwd, arms fwd, palms up
- 3-4: 2 running steps in place LR, arms down
- 5-6: 2 running steps fwd LR
- 7: Leap on L fwd and 1/4 turn to left side (face CW)
- 8: R stamps next to L
- 9: R to right side big step
- 10: Hold
- 11: L to left side
- 12: Close R to L
- 13: L to left side
- 14: Leap on R while turning 3/4 to left side, end up facing center

15:     L in place
16:     Close R to L

PART THREE
1-2:   Arms on each other's shoulders. Balance R
3-4:   Balance L
5:      Face CCW. Leap R fwd
6:      Run L fwd
7:      Leap R fwd
8:      Run L fwd
9-16:   Repeat 1-8

HAROA HAKTANA
(Little Shepherdess)

Dance: Jonathan Karmon
Music: Willensky
Tikva LP 69

Formation: Circle, face center, arms down close to body

PART ONE
1-2: Step-hop on R to right side and 1/2 turn to right
3-4: Step-hop on L to left side and 1/2 turn to left
5-6: Step-hop on R to right side and 1/2 turn to left
7-8: Step-hop on L to left side and 1/2 turn to right
9-10: Step-hop on R to right side and 1/2 turn to right
11-12: Step-hop on L to left side and 1/2 turn to right (face center)
13-14: Balance R, raise hands and snap fingers
15-16: Balance L and snap fingers
17-32: Repeat 1-16

PART TWO
1-2: Step-hop on R in place and 1/4 turn to R (face CCW)
3-4: Step-hop on L to left side
5-6: Step-hop on R to right side and 1/2 turn to left (face CW)
7-8: Step-hop on L to left side and 1/4 turn to right (face center)
9-12: Repeat counts 13-16 Part One
13-24: Repeat 1-12
25-26: Step-hop on R in place. Kick L fwd, arms fwd, palms up
27-28: 2 running steps in place LR, arms down
29-32: Reverse 25-28

MAMTERA (Sprinkler) Dance: Shmuel Cohen (Vicky)
Music: Willensky
Tikva LP 69

Formation: Circle, hold hands, face CCW

PART ONE
1-2:   Step-hop R fwd
3-4:   Step-hop L fwd
5-6:   Step-hop R fwd
7-10:   Mayim step L
11-12: L crosses in front of R and hop on L
13:     Face center. R to right side
14:     Close L to R
15-16: Repeat 13-14
17-18: Step-hop on R to right side
19-24: Reverse 13-18, start L to left side
25-48: Repeat 1-24

PART TWO
1-2:   Release hands. Two steps in place RL at the same time
        one complete turn to right side. End up facing center
3:      Jump on both feet
4:      Hop on L
5:      R fwd, arms fwd, and palms up
6:      L bwd, arms down
7:      Jump on both feet
8:      Hop on L
9-16:   Repeat 1-8

PART THREE
1-2:   Join hands. Face CCW. Step-hop R fwd
3-4:   Step-hop L fwd
5:      Jump on both feet

6:      Leap R bwd
7-8:   Step-hop L bwd
9-16:   Repeat 1-8

PART FOUR
1:      Face center. R to right side (stamp)
2:      Hold
3-5:   Yem L
6-7:   Two steps in place RL (stamp)
8:      Hold
9-16:   Repeat 1-8

PART FIVE
1-16:   Repeat Part Three

EREV BA (Evening Is Setting)   Dance: Yoav Ashriel
                                    Music: Levanon
                                    Tikva LP 98

Formation: Circle, face center, join hands

PART ONE
   1:      R to right side
   2:      L crosses in front of R
   3:      R bwd
   4:      L to left side
   5-7:   Face CW. 3 steps fwd RLR
   8:      Pause
   9:      L bwd
   10:     Face center. R swd
   11-14: Mayim step L
   15:     L crosses in front of R
   16:     Pause
   17-32: Repeat 1-16

PART TWO
   1-2:   Release hands. Travel to right side with 2 steps RL
           while completing a right turn, once around
   3:      R to right side
   4:      L crosses in front of R
   5:      R bwd
   6-8:   Reverse 3-5, start L to left side
   9-16:   Repeat 1-8

PART THREE
   1:      Face CW. R to right side, arms open
   2:      L crosses in front of R, cross arms, and snap fingers
   3-6:   Repeat 1-2 twice more
   7:      R to right side

8:     L to left side
9:     R crosses in front of L, cross arms, and snap fingers
10:    L to left side, open arms
11-14: Repeat 9-10 twice more. On last step face center
15-16: Repeat 1-2 Part Two

LECH, LECH LAMIDBAR
(Go to the Desert)

Dance: Folk
Music: Argon
Israel LP 5/6

Formation: Circle, face center, join hands

PART ONE
1:     Leap on R to right side
2:     L crosses in front of R
3:     Close R to L
4:     Pause
5:     L to left side
6:     Close R to L, bend knees. Release hands and clap
7-8:   Repeat 5-6
9-32: Repeat 1-8 three more times

PART TWO
1-2:   Join hands. Step-hop R in place, kick L in front of R
3-4:   Step-hop L in place, kick R in front of L
5-8:   Mayim step R. Move to left side
9-32: Repeat 1-8 three more times

PART THREE
1-2:   Step-bend R to right side
3-4:   Step-bend L to left side
5:     R fwd. Arms bent fwd
6:     L bwd
7:     Close R to L and arms down
8:     Pause
9-16: Repeat 1-8

PART FOUR
1-4:   Mayim step R
5:     R crosses in front of L

    6:      L to left side
    7:      R crosses behind L
    8:      Hop on R
 9-16:   Reverse 1-8, start L to right side
17-32: Repeat 1-16

2 Couple Dances

VEDAVID YEFE EYNAIM
(And David Was Fair to Behold)

Dance: Rivka Sturman
Music: Shelem
Tikva LP 138

Formation: Couples in a circle facing CCW, boys inside, girls outside, join inside hands

1-4:   4 steps fwd, start R
5-8:   4 steps, start R. Boy walks bwd, girl in place. All end up in one big circle and join hands
9-12: 4 steps fwd, start R, raise arms
13-16: 4 steps bwd, start R, arms down. Release hands
17-24: Girls 4 steps fwd and 4 steps bwd, start R while boy stands in place and claps each count
25-28: Boys 4 steps fwd, start R. On last step make 1/2 turn to right side. Girls clap 4 times in place
29-32: Boys 4 steps fwd, start R. Don't return to own partner. Move to left side which means change partners. Girls stand still
33-40: Right arm around each other's waist, left arms up. Pivot on inside foot (8 steps)

ZEMER ATIK (Ancient Song)   Dance: Rivka Sturman
                                Music: Neeman
                                Tikva LP 138

Formation: Couples in a circle, girl in front of boy, all facing
            CCW, left arm is bent and touches own left
            shoulder, right arm is extended fwd and joins left
            hand of the person in front

PART ONE
  1-4:   4 steps fwd RLRL
  5:      Release hands. R to right side
  6:      Bend right knee and clap over right shoulder
  7-8:   Reverse 5-6
  9-32:   Repeat 1-8 three more times

PART TWO
Face center of circle
  33:     R fwd
  34:     Bend right knee and snap fingers over right shoulder
  35-36: Reverse 1-2
  37-40: 4 steps bwd RLRL, lower arms gradually
  41-64: Repeat 1-8 three more times

PART THREE
Music starts from the beginning, couples side by side facing
CCW, boy inside, girl outside, join inside hands
  1-4:   4 steps fwd RLRL
  5-6:   R fwd and turn toward each other
  7-8:   Close R to L and bow
  9-32:   Repeat 1-8 three more times

PART FOUR

33:    R fwd

34:    Bend right knee

35:    L fwd

36:    Bend left knee

37-40: Lift inside arms. Four steps in place RLRL. Girl while walking takes a 1/2 turn to left side, she faces CW

41-44: Boy brings his right arm down with girl's left behind her head. Her right arm extends behind partner's back. In this position both move CW with steps from 1-4

45-48: 4 steps RLRL coming back to place, both side by side, face CCW

49-64: Repeat 33-48. On last steps girl ends up in front of boy and is ready to start the dance from the beginning

DAYAGIM (Fishermen)

Dance: Shalom Hermon
Music: Aldema
Tikva LP 80

Formation: Couples in circle, girls on boys' right, facing CCW, arms in skating position behind body

PART ONE
1-4: 4 running steps fwd LRLR. Release hands
5-8: *Boy—* Step-hop L diagonally to left side. Step-hop R diagonally to right side
      Girl— Step-hop L crosses over R in front. Step-hop R crosses over L in front
9-12: Join hands, skating position in front of body. Repeat count 1-4
13-16: *Boy—* 2 slow stamping steps in place LR
        Girl— L to left side, in front of boy. Leap on R making a full turn, ending up inside of the circle, and 2 steps in place LR
17-20: Repeat count 1-4
21-24: Release hands
        Boy— Girl's step, count 5-8
        Girl— Boy's step, count 5-8
25-32: Partners face each other. 8 running steps, start L, right arms around each other's waist, left arms raised, 1-1/2 turns CW. Boy ends up inside with back to center, girl faces center

PART TWO
Arms are bent at shoulder level, partners touch each other's palms
1: *Boy—* L to left side
2:          Bend left knee
3:          R to right side

4:          Bend right knee
        Girl—   Reverse steps
5-8:   Arms down
        Boy—   Run 4 steps L R L R, change places with girl
                on right side, passing her with right shoulder,
                meeting a third person
        Girl—   Reverse, girl inside of circle, boy outside
9-16:   Repeat count 1-8. On last count, girl takes 2 steps.
        Face own partner
17-20:   Join both hands
        Boy—   Step-hop fwd L. Step-hop fwd R
        Girl—   Step-hop bwd L. Step-hop bwd R
21-24:   Repeat steps 17-20 but reverse direction
25-32:   Arms in skating position behind body. Pivot around
        with 8 steps, turn CCW, start L. End up in beginning
        position, both facing CCW

KESCHOSHANA BEIN HACHOCHIM
(As a Lily among Thorns)

Dance: Yaacov Levy
Music: Hadar
Tikva LP 117

Formation: Couples, side by side, facing CCW, boy inside,
girl outside, join inside hands, start with outside
foot, boy L, girl R. Boy's steps are described

PART ONE
1-2:   L fwd, step-bend
3-4:   R fwd, step-bend
5-8:   Repeat 1-4
9-11: Partners face each other. Yem L
12:    Hop on L
13:    R to right side
14:    L crosses in front of R
15:    Hop on L
16:    R to right side
17-32: Repeat 1-16

PART TWO
1-2:   Face CCW. Step-hop L fwd
3-4:   Step-hop R fwd
5-6:   Step-hop L fwd. On hop release hands and 1/4 turn to
left side. Partners are back to back
7:     R touches the floor. Bend and clap
8:     Pause
9-12: Reverse 1-4, start with R fwd
13-14: Step-hop R fwd. On hop 1/4 turn to right side.
Partners face each other
15:    L touches the floor. At the same time boy's right
hand claps girl's left
16:    Pause
17-32: Repeat 1-16

DODI-LI (My Beloved Is Mine)   Dance: Rivka Sturman
                                     Music: Chen
                                     Tikva LP 138

Formation: Couples face each other, boy with back to center, girl faces center, boy's right hand joins girl's left, partners start with opposite foot. Boy's steps are described

CHORUS
- 1-3:   Yem L
- 4:   Pivot on L, face CCW
- 5:   R fwd
- 6:   Hold
- 7-10: Tcherkessia L. On first step bend both arms fwd and bend left knee. On third step arms down. On fourth step pivot on R. Face each other again
- 11:   L in place
- 12:   Hold
- 13-16: Yem R
- 17-32: Repeat 1-16

PART ONE
- 1-5:   Repeat 1-5 Chorus
- 6:   Pivot R, 1/2 turn to right side. Release hands. Both face CW
- 7-10: Join inside hands. 4 steps bwd LRLR. On last step pivot on R. End up facing each other again
- 11-16: Join original hands and repeat 11-16 Chorus
- 17-32: Repeat 1-16

REPEAT CHORUS

PART TWO

1-6: Repeat 1-6 Part One but do not change hands

7-8: 2 steps bwd LR. On second step pivot on R, 1/2 turn to left side. Face CCW

9-10: 2 steps fwd LR. On last step pivot on R, 1/4 turn to right side. Partners face each other again

11-16: Repeat 11-16 Chorus

17-32: Repeat 1-16

REPEAT CHORUS

PART THREE

1-5: Repeat 1-5 Chorus

6: Pivot on R, end up facing each other

7-10: Mayim step L (move CW)

11: L crosses in front of R

12: Hold

13-16: Yem R

17-32: Repeat 1-16

KRAKOVIAK

Music and Dance: Folk
Electra LP 186

Formation: Couples in a circle face CCW, girl outside, boy inside, join inside hands. Boy's steps are described. Girl, opposite foot

PART ONE
- 1-2: Balance L, away from each other
- 3-4: Balance R, toward each other
- 5-8: Repeat 1-4
- 9-10: 2 running steps fwd L R
- 11: Jump on both feet
- 12: Release hands. Hop on L and 1/2 turn to right side (face CW)
- 13-16: Reverse 9-12, start R, move CW

PART TWO
- 1-4: Face CCW, repeat 1-4 Part One
- 5-16: Partners face each other. Boy puts his hands on girl's waist, girl puts her hands on his shoulders. In this position they execute 6 step-hops while turning CW at the same time moving CCW. Boy starts L, girl R

This is one of many variations

EZ VAKEVEZ
(The Goat and the Sheep Are Shorn)

Dance: Yoav Ashriel
Music: Shelem
Tikva LP 69

Formation: Couples face each other, boys face CCW, girls CW
in a circle, right arms are bent fwd, join hands,
left arms up. Part One and Part Three start with
same foot

PART ONE
1-4: 4 running steps fwd (girl bwd)
5: R fwd, toward each other
6: Leap on L, change places at the same time passing
right shoulders
7: Jump on both feet
8: Hop on L
9-16: Repeat 1-8, reverse direction, move CW. On last count
release hands, boy faces center of circle

PART TWO
Step for boy
1: R to right side
2: Hold
3: Leap on L to left side
4: Stamp R next to L
5: R to right side
6: 1/2 turn to right side on R
7: L to left side
8: 1/2 turn to left side on L
9-16: Repeat 1-8
Step for girl
1: Arms down, palms fwd. R fwd, arms fwd
2: L bwd on toe, arms down
3-6: Repeat 1-2 two more times

7:    R bwd, arms bwd
8:    L fwd, arms down
9-16: Repeat 1-8

PART THREE
Partners face each other as in Part One, join both hands, keep
knees bent for next four measures
1:    Leap R fwd (girl bwd)
2:    Close L to R
3:    Right heel touches floor, next to L
4:    Right toe touches floor
5-16: Repeat 1-4 three more times
17-24: Partners face each other. Bring right arms around each
       other's waist, left arms up. 8 pivot steps moving CW
25-32: Reverse 17-24, left arms around waists. Pivot CCW

BAT YIFTACH
(Daughter of Jephta)

Dance: Shalom Hermon
Music: Neeman
Israel LP 7

Formation: Couples in a circle, facing CCW, boy inside, girl
outside, boy extends his right arm behind
partner's shoulder, girl extends her left arm in
front of boy, they join both hands

PART ONE
1-2: Step-bend R fwd
3-4: Step-bend L fwd
5: Brush R fwd
6: Hop on L
7-8: Repeat 5-6
9-14: Repeat 1-6
15: Close R to L
16: Pause
17-32: Repeat 1-16

PART TWO
1-2: Run 2 steps fwd RL
3: Jump on both feet
4: Hop on L
5-8: Repeat 1-4
9-14: 6 running steps in place, start R. At the same time one
complete turn CCW
15: Face CCW. Jump on both feet
16: Hop on L
17-32: Repeat 1-16. On last 2 counts release hands. Both end
up facing center of circle, girl behind boy

PART THREE

Step for boy

  1-8:   4 step-bend fwd, start R, hands up, clap on each bend

  9-20: 6 step-bend bwd, start R, clap on each bend

21-24: 2 step-bend fwd, start R, clap on each bend

Step for girl

  1-8:   8 pivot steps in place 1 3/4 turns to right side. End up with right shoulder to center, face CW

  9-10: Run fwd RL

11:      Jump on both feet

12:      Hop on L and 1/2 turn to right side, facing CCW

13-16: Repeat 9-12, on last count 1/4 turn to left, face center

17-20: Run 4 steps fwd, passing partners right. On last step 1/2 turn to left side, face partner

21-22: 2 running steps fwd RL, toward partner

23-24: Jump and hop on L, in front of partner

25-32: Both right arms around each other's waist, left arms up. 8 pivot steps turning in place CW

33-64: Repeat 1-32

3 Line Dances

SHIRU HASHIR (Sing the Song)   Dance: Leah Bergstein
                                    Music: Shelem
                                    Tikva LP 117

Formation: Line, join hands, face CCW

PART ONE
  1-2:   Body down. Run fwd 2 steps, RL
  3-6:   Body up. Run 4 steps from side to side, R to right side and L to left side, RLRL
  7-8:   Step-hop on R in place, at the same time extending L fwd
  9-11: Run 3 steps bwd, LRL
  12-13: Step-hop on R in place, at the same time extending L fwd
  14:    Run 2 steps in place, LR
  15:    L in place
  16-30: Repeat 1-15

PART TWO
Face center
  1:     Tap right heel in place
  2:     Leap on R in place
  3-4:   Repeat 1-2 with L
  5-8:   Repeat 1-4
  9:     Step on R fwd. Body bends down and arms swing bwd
  10:    Pause
  11-12: Step-hop on L bwd. Body up and arms swing up
  13-24: Repeat 9-12 three more times. Travel gradually to right side while doing 9-24

25-30: Double Tcherkessia, start R
31: R crosses over L in front
32: L bwd and 1/4 turn to right, facing CCW
33: Run R fwd
34: Run L fwd and 1/2 turn to left, facing CW
35: Leap on R bwd, arms swing up
36: L bwd and 1/2 turn to right, facing CCW, arms down

HINE MA TOV (How Good It Is) Dance: Rivka Sturman
Music: Jacobson
Tikva LP 138

Formation: Line, join hands, face CCW

CHORUS
 1-2:   Step-bend R fwd
 3-8:   3 more step-bend fwd LRL
 9-16: 8 running steps fwd, start R
17-32: Repeat 1-16

PART ONE
 1:     Face center. R to right side
 2:     Hold
 3:     L bwd, arms bwd
 4:     Close R to L
 5:     L fwd, arms up high
 6:     Hold
 7:     Close R to L
 8:     Hold
 9-12: Yem R
13-16: Yem L
17-32: Repeat 1-16

REPEAT CHORUS

PART TWO
 1-8:   Face center. 8 running steps fwd, start R, lift arms up
        high gradually
 9-12: Yem R
13-16: Yem L
17-24: 8 running steps bwd, start R, arms down gradually
25-32: Repeat 9-16

DEBKA RAFIACH

Dance and music: Folk
Tikva LP 80

Formation: Line, hold hands, face center, move CCW

PART ONE
- 1: Right heel fwd, touches floor
- 2: Hold
- 3: R touches next to L
- 4: Hold
- 5: Right heel fwd, touches floor
- 6: Hold
- 7: Close R to L
- 8: 1/4 turn on R to right side
- 9: L fwd
- 10: 1/4 turn on L to left side
- 11: Close R to L
- 12: Hold
- 13-16: Bounce 4 times, just raising heels off floor
- 17-32: Repeat 1-16

PART TWO
- 1: R points in front over L
- 2: 1/4 turn on L to right side
- 3: R fwd
- 4: Hold
- 5: L fwd
- 6: 1/4 turn on L to left side
- 7: Close R to L
- 8: Hold
- 9-48: Repeat 1-8 five more times

PART THREE
1-4: Jump 4 times, feet together
5: R stamps fwd. Right shoulder fwd, bend down
6: Stamp again, R fwd
7: Close R to L, body raises
8: 1/4 turn on R to right side
9: L fwd and 1/4 turn to left side
10: R to right side
11: Close L to R
12: Hold

PART FOUR
1: R to right side, turn head to right side and right shoulder fwd
2: L crosses behind R, shoulder bwd
3-8: Repeat 1-2 three more times
9-16: Repeat 1-8 but turn head to left side on count 9
17-32: Repeat 1-16

PART FIVE
1: R stamps in front over L, bend down, right shoulder fwd
2: 1/4 turn on L to left side
3-4: Face CCW. Step-hop fwd on R
5-7: 3 steps fwd LRL
8: 1/4 turn on L to left side
9-48: Repeat 1-8 five more times

PART SIX
1: Face CW. R stamps to right side, body down
2: Stamp R again and 1/2 turn on R to right side, body up
3: Face CCW. L stamps to left side
4: Stamp L again and 1/2 turn on L to left side
5-8: Repeat 1-4

9: Face center. Jump both feet apart, R in front, L bwd (lunge)
10: Reverse jump, L in front, R bwd
11: Jump and close feet
12: Hold

This description is one of many variations

DEBKA DRUZ

Dance: Shmuel Cohen
Music: Givon
Tikva LP 100

Formation: Line, face and move CCW, bend left arm behind touching body, right arm extends fwd, join hands

CHORUS
1-2: L fwd
3-4: R fwd
5-6: Point L fwd
7-8: Point L swd
9-32: Repeat 1-8 three more times. On last beat shift weight on L

PART ONE
33-34: Leap on R to right side, landing with right knee bent. At the same time L is bent off the floor in front of R, flex foot
35-36: Stretch L sharply to left side, at the same time accent with R
37: Left heel touches the floor
38: Leap on L to left side
39: Close R to L with stamp
40: Hold
41-64: Repeat 33-40 three more times

REPEAT CHORUS

PART TWO
33-34: L fwd
35-36: Close R to L
37-38: L swd
39-40: Close R to L

41-48: Repeat 33-40 Part One
49-64: Repeat 33-48

REPEAT CHORUS

PART THREE
33:      Left heel touches fwd
34:      Leap on L fwd
35:      Close R to L
36:      Hold
37-40: Repeat 33-36
41-42: Jump on both feet
43-44: Hop on R
45-48: Repeat 33-36
49-56: Repeat 33-40
57-58: Jump on both feet
59-60: Jump on both feet
61-63: 3 stamps in place RLR, body bends down
64:      Hold

REPEAT CHORUS

PART FOUR
Face center
33:      Left heel touches floor to left side
34:      Leap on L to left side .
35:      R crosses in front of left, both knees are bent (squat),
         arms up
36:      Hold
37:      L bwd
38-39: R circles in front of L to right side, knee bent and foot
         flexed, arms move down gradually
40:      R to right side
41-64: Repeat 33-40 three more times

DEBKAT HABIR (Heroic Debka)

Dance: Moshe Levy
Music: Sharabi
Tikva LP 69

Formation: Line, face circle center, close to each other, join hands, and bend arms fwd

PART ONE
1-5: 5 bounces, bend and stretch knees
6: Jump off both feet
7: Hop on L and R fwd straight, heel touches floor
8: Close R to L
9-32: Repeat 1-8 three more times

PART TWO
1-2: Release arms, cross behind back. Face CCW. Step-hop on R, kick L to left side
3: L crosses behind R
4: R crosses in front of L
5-8: Reverse 1-4
9-32: Repeat 1-8 three more times

PART THREE
1: Join hands. R fwd
2: Hold
3: L fwd
4: Hold
5: R fwd
6: L bwd
7: Brush R bwd
8: Leap on R bwd
9: L crosses behind R (ball of L hits the floor)
10: Hold
11-12: Bounce twice

13:     Hop on R to left side
14:     Leap on L to left side
15:     Close R to L
16:     Hold
17-32: Repeat 1-16

PART FOUR

1:     Face center. Arms on each other's shoulders. R to right side
2:     Hold
3:     L crosses behind R
4:     Hold
5-12: Repeat 1-4 twice more
13-14: Fast Yem R. On third step kick L fwd
15:     Leap on left, at the same time kick R fwd (change feet in the air)
16:     Close R to L
17-32: Repeat 1-16

PART FIVE

1:     R to right side
2:     1/2 turn to right side on R. End up with back to center
3:     Join hands. L to left side
4:     Hold
5:     R crosses behind L
6:     L to left side
7:     Hop on L
8:     R crosses behind L
9-16: Reverse 1-8. Start L to left side
17-32: Repeat 1-16

PART SIX

1:	Face CCW. Join hands. R fwd
2:	Hold
3:	Brush L fwd
4:	Leap on L fwd
5:	R bwd
6:	Hold
7:	Close L to R
8:	Hold
9-11:	Repeat 1-3
12:	Hop on R
13:	L fwd
14:	R bwd
15:	Close L to R
16:	Hold
17-32:	Repeat 1-16

DEBKA DAYAGIM
(Fishermen's Debka)

Dance: Shalom Hermon
Music: Aldema
Tikva LP 100

Formation: Line, join hands, face and move CCW

PART ONE
1-2: 2 running steps fwd RL, body bent down
3-8: Body raises. 3 step-hops fwd RLR
9-16: Reverse 1-8. Start with L
17-18: Face center. Step-hop on R in place, kick L fwd. Arms up
19-20: Step-hop on L in place, kick R bwd. Arms down
21-24: Repeat 17-20
25-32: Repeat 17-24 but L crosses over R in front (travel to left side)
33-48: Repeat 1-16

PART TWO
Face center
1-6: Double Tcherkessia, start R over L in front
7-8: Step-hop on R fwd
9-10: Step-hop L crosses over R in front
11-12: Step-hop on R bwd
13-14: Step-hop on L to left side
15-16: Step-hop on R in place
17-18: Hop twice on R in place, point L fwd
19-20: Hop twice on R in place, point L to left side
21-22: Close L to R